PRUNING IN A PANDEMIC

A
poetic
journey
through a
perilous time

Marco Fortino

Pruning in a Pandemic

tellwell

Tellwell Talent
www.tellwell.ca

ISBN
978-0-2288-6172-0 (Hardcover)
978-0-2288-6173-7 (Paperback)

To my incredibly supportive wife Patricia,
and my two amazing sons, Francesco and Gianluca.
I love all of you to the moon and back.

Table of Contents

FIVE

SIX

SEVEN

EPILOGUE

eternal darkness
calls me like a siren
but I will not heed its cry—
at least not yet

ONE

FOOTSTEPS IN THE DARK

relentlessly they march
through my mind
from the past
into the ever present
torturing my imagination
where they will lead
I suspect I know
but from that place
there will be no
safe passage home
patiently I wait here
alone in the dark
hoping for a glimmer
of light

THE POET AT THE WINDOW

he peers anxiously
at the embattled sky
that has quickly formed
above the sullen landscape
but in those clouds
he discerns a message
that he must urgently
transmit to paper
before the tempest
arrives and erases
their celestial directive

THE GLASS REFUGE

into the glass refuge
I come seeking solace
from the death found
outside covered
in a blanket of white

verdant foliage
climbs to the top
of its glass cage
obliviously mocking
the bare branches
trapped outside
in a snowy prison

taking place unnoticed
in a public square
a battle rages
between death and freedom

TWO

LONG BEFORE PANDEMICS

the virus
was born
in the veins
of humankind
poisoning all
they touched
and bringing
death and destruction
upon themselves
and their neighbours
wiping out
much more
than one
tiny pathogen
could ever
dream of destroying

HISTORY NEVER DIES

The experts claim
the Crusades
ended centuries ago,
but bombs blast
and people die.
Holy War rages on
in cities and
the countryside.
The only constant
being death that links
centuries and cultures
in a deadly embrace,
appearing as a bloody
collage on a canvas
made of human hide.

ETERNAL ENEMY

Never start a
fight with a foe
who has a
long memory.
For much longer
than both of you
shall live
will your
children and
their children
continue to
fight, until
there is no one
left to hate
and no one
left to die.

JESUS AND MUHAMMAD

What if
they lived
amongst us?
Would they
be friends?
Would they
be online?
Would they
have millions
of followers?
Would their
messages go viral?
What would
they say
to each other
about all the
death and destruction
wrought in
their names?
My guess is
there would be
no words shared,
only tears.

THREE

NEWS FROM THE FRONT

In an age
of technical marvel
entire nations
are on lockdown.

A tiny superbug
has an entire
self-isolated world
on the edge
of their seats
two metres apart.

All while some
leaders
are showing courage
and others
are in denial.

TINY PATHOGEN

one thousandth the size
of a hair follicle
and yet
it has shut down
the world's metropolises
leaving countries
with no visible
enemy to attack
forcing them
to build walls
to protect themselves
from their own
fear and hatred

FOR THE BASEBALL FAN

The games are gone
but there is no
shortage of stats
during a pandemic.
Whereas before
one was preoccupied
with ERAs and RBIs,
now every fan is
glued to the screen
checking the stats:
for those infected,
for those severely ill,
for those recently deceased.

PRUNING IN A PANDEMIC

The humble pruner,
removing the dead
and unneeded branches
to encourage new life,
looks upward
at his next cut
and the sun
temporarily blinds him.

While from above,
the Master Pruner
looks down pensively,
as He too
prepares to make
His next cuts
to promote new life.

FOUR

AUTUMN LEAVES

one leaf at a time
falling from the tree of life
longing for winter

THESE HANDS

once playful and smooth
now gnarled and without strength
fast losing their grip

AT THE HOME

by the window I
wait for someone to appear
and brighten my soul

WHAT IF?

My weakness
makes you strong?
My pain serves
as your muse?
My unintelligible
speech helps clarify?

I sit here
as the hours
drag by
wondering about
my purpose.
I look at
your confused faces
and decide you
have no clue,
but I continue
to sit here
wondering—
what if?

FOR MY SAFETY

Here I am
locked inside
my own
four walls.

For my safety,
they say.

I lived freely
through the
Great Depression and
World War II.

Before heading
for shelter,
we'd run to the
nearest hilltop
to see the
enemy bombers
drop their death
on the distant
countryside.

I never
thought about
my safety then.

Now I sit
here almost ninety,
all alone
in this cell,
but safe.

THROUGH THE GLASS

as tears stream
down her face
I struggle to cry out
but she cannot hear
even though we are only
a foot apart this
glass wall makes it seem
as distant as a mile
for infection threatens
us both and has
diminished these visits
offering only partial
relief from the dreary
boredom and solitude
of life spent in safety
from one another

LIFE IN THE THROES OF DEATH

shut out
from the life
they know
they are moved
to open
their doors
and step onto
their tri-coloured
balconies
singing and clapping
their way
through their ordeal
undaunted by death
but
inspired by life
and its
unlikely heroes

TEMPORARY HEROES

Remember when
we walked the
streets with pride?

How we were
accompanied by
great cheers
coming from the
tri-coloured balconies
above?

Now we are seen
as messengers of woe,
carriers of death,
cursed at and shunned.

We sought no
part of this
faulty pedestal.

We only strove to
do our work and
serve those who
would now cast
us out.

THE QUARANTINE BLUES

Where I come from
there is no choice;
work the land or
starve to death.
When my land had
no more to give,
we headed north
to work the earth
and share the rewards
with those patient
but hungry mouths
waiting back home.
All was fine until
a silent killer appeared
and forced us
off the soil.
Now,
with fourteen guys,
for fourteen days,
we sit and wait
and sing the
Quarantine Blues.

BORN IN THE TIME OF PLAGUE

O beautiful girl!
O beautiful boy!
Born into this
new and fearful world.

Will you grow up
afraid of the other?
Will you ever know
the joy of playing
with your friends
in the park?
Will the pre-pandemic
world appear only as
a fantasyland where
people used to
live and love
unafraid of spreading
infection?

O beautiful girl!
O beautiful boy!
Will you ever know?

FIVE

THE TRUTH

It is dying
a slow
and deliberate
death here
in the twenty-first century.

The trend
that is all the rage
has people creating
their own truths when
the absolute one
is either too
inconvenient or too
time-consuming
to discover.

Unscrupulous rulers
especially
relish this anti-truth age
because it sets them
free from accountability
and renders
that pesky entity known
as a conscience
moot.

PANDEMIC DEADLINE

it's upsetting
when crises refuse
to cooperate
with our own agendas
how inconvenient
when the number
of lives lost continue
to mount
and our plans
lay in waste
how especially frustrating
for those in power
who are not used
to being told no
or worse yet
being told
to be patient and resolute

PRELUDE TO A POLICE STATE

as a tiny superbug
wreaks its havoc
millions of people
are rendered
captive

flights have stopped
and borders have
been shut
curfews have been
imposed

talk of army and
police to enforce
the laws of the land
swirl about
while the tiny superbug
continues to roam
completely free

THE CAPTAIN WAS TOLD

to follow
the chain
of command
even if it
led to
unnecessary death

for national
security they
argued or
could have been
fear of the
commander-in-chief

as a sacrifice
to the gods
of officialdom
the captain
was cast out

he left in triumph
to the cheers
of loyal troops
who clearly knew
the leader
among them

BLAME SHIFTER

in love with
his own image
to the detriment
of all others
our modern
day Narcissus-
in-power
believes no one
can contradict
him because
he alone
understands and
he alone
commands
an army of sycophants
who will
do anything
to keep him
on his self-constructed
pedestal

WHAT GOES AROUND

from their hilltop
they proclaimed
against the
foreigner

build walls
close borders
"they are
pariahs!"

until one
day a tiny
superbug
came to visit

now they sit
on their lonely perch
with their
neighbours aghast

the world looks
at this once
proud people and proclaims
"they are pariahs!"

SIX

I AM NOT THE VIRUS

But you treat
me as such,
disinfecting
everything I
touch.

Every person
I have seen
is a suspect
in your eyes,
an accomplice
I have recruited
to ensure
your demise.

Your smile
and a few
kind words,
the fact
does not allay,
you prefer to be
a safe two metres away.

One day soon
we may embrace,
but will you
still see me
as the virus'
face?

THE NEW HATERS

I remember
a time not
so long ago
when haters
were confined
to the dark crevices
of their minds.
Sure, they could
conspire to meet
other like-minded
souls and certainly
inflict plenty of hate,
but flash forward
to the twenty-first
century and these
purveyors of hate
can reach millions
of their fellow
worshippers of darkness
in an instant,
all with a click.

VIRUSES GONE VIRAL

mid 2020 and
Covid-19
is all the rage
but not to be
outdone ageless
viruses strike back

hatred and prejudice
will not be denied

eight minutes and
forty-six seconds
lapse and the
masses leave their
quiet self-isolation
to protest

only to meet with
counter protesters
spewing their hate
in a never-ending
cycle of hatred
and distrust

A SIMPLE CRY

while face down
on the pavement
the man uttered
the now famous words

"I can't breathe"

less than
nine minutes later
he would be
heard no more

soon an entire
nation gasped
for air and
wondered if it
would ever breathe
peacefully again

AS THE COUNTRY BURNS

the leader
stokes the flames
but when it gets hot
he runs and hides
while the brave
stay behind
and work
on the mending
of a once great
nation that
was brought
to its knees
by hatred
and ignorance

THE SHINING CITY

it was to
be built on
a hill as a
beacon for all

four
hundred years ago
a fledgling nation
set this as
their goal

flash forward to
present day
and the lustre
has faded

in its place
torn dreams
of a people desperately
seeking a way back
to that long abandoned
hilltop

SEVEN

WITH MY NEW APP

travelling at the speed
of touch
I can travel
the world
from the comfort
of my kitchen table
casually eavesdropping
on nations unaware
of the mystery visitor
in their world of shut-ins
held captive
by a far more sinister
silent interloper
who cannot
be powered off

A PRAYER FOR WORLD PEACE

As a child
and as an
adult
I have often
prayed for
world peace.
I had
abandoned all hope
when providentially,
or by pure dumb luck,
the earth was sent
a precious gift
in the form of a tiny
pathogen, which
startled all
those whom Hubris
had blinded and
provided them a chance
to work together
for the greater good,
assuming they had
the will and courage
to do so.

ALL HAIL THE SPARROW

on my porch
oblivious to
death in the air
the sparrows
continue to
plan for their
spring home
one twig at
a time
all the while
laughing at
the peril that
has all of us
enclosed
in our own nests

FROM MY CONTROL CENTRE

from my
control centre
that is my
kitchen table
the future
appears uncertain
and wrought
with peril
until I peer into
the hopeful eyes
of my boys
providing for me
a portal
to a constellation
of unsurpassed
brightness and promise

THE POET GARDENER

through the
windowpane
the poet gardener
looks wistfully
at his
snow-covered
garden

dreams of tilling
and sowing fills
the imagination
as do visions of new life
emanating from
the dormant earth

glancing back to
his desk
the poet gardener
realizes as he
sees the blank page
that new life
is also possible
in the dead of winter

MAGNOLIA BLOSSOMS

in a world
marked by
death and
social upheaval
these bursts
of vibrant pinks
and purples
serve as a reminder
of nature's grandeur
and resilience
persevering through
another cold and
dark winter
urging us
to sprout from
our self-imposed dormancy
both stronger and wiser
while bringing
our own sense
of beauty and life
to this quiet
and isolated earth

EPILOGUE

215 PLUS

as an ally
not a saviour
I stand here
with you
in quiet reverence
as I stare
at all these shoes
left in tribute
for those who
can no longer
fill them
for those whose dreams
and identities
were torn from them
by the architects
of a system
meant to assimilate
rather than to educate
and though I
can never know
the pain
I can and must
stand up
and offer
my humble hands
to help
in any way
you choose

Acknowledgements

I would like to thank the entire team at Tellwell Talent whose professionalism and support was especially appreciated by this fledgling writer. In addition, special thanks to my family who provided their feedback and encouragement throughout this journey.

CPSIA information can be obtained
at www.ICGtesting.com
Printed in the USA
LVHW091406081221
705193LV00030B/178

9 780228 861720